Teacher Take-Out
for Preschoolers

12 Complete Lessons for Teachers on the Go!

Created by **M**elinda **M**ahand

4360-23

©1997 Broadman & Holman Supplies, Nashville, TN, printed in USA.

The Man Who Ate Bugs and Honey

What is your favorite thing to eat for breakfast? What is your favorite thing to eat for dinner?

The Bible tells about a man named John. John did not eat the kind of food you eat. John ate locusts and honey. A locust is kind of like a grasshopper. John did not wear the kind of clothes you wear either. His clothes were made of camel's hair. Around his waist, he tied a leather belt.

John taught the people about Jesus. But John did not teach inside a church or inside a school like your teachers do. John taught outside near a river. People came from all over the land of Judea to hear John teach.

"I have come to tell you about Jesus," John said to all the people. "Jesus is God's Son. He is coming soon."

One day while John was teaching, a man came walking by. Do you know who the man was? The man was Jesus. Jesus was coming to be baptized. John and Jesus waded out into the Jordan River. John baptized Jesus in the cool river water.

When Jesus came out of the water, He heard God say: "You are My Son. I love You."

John was glad he had told the people about Jesus.

From Mark 1:1-11

Bible Song Time
By the River
(tune "Row Your Boat")

By the river, what did John eat? (Pretend to eat.)
He ate locusts and some honey sweet.

By the river, what did John wear? (Pat shirt.)
He wore clothing made from camel's hair.

By the river, what did John say? (Cup hands around ears.)
Jesus, God's Son, will come here some day. (Point toward heaven.)

Bible Fun Time
Take a River Walk

Locate a jump rope or a long strand of yarn. Comment: "People came from all around to hear John teach. As people walked to the river, they might have had to duck under a tree limb or hop over a ditch. We can pretend to walk to the river, too. Let's see how many different ways we can move as we go." A teacher or a child can help you move the rope as the preschoolers take turns following these instructions:

- "Step over the rope." (Hold the rope two inches off the floor.)
- "Duck under the rope." (Hold the rope two feet off the floor.)
- "Walk on the rope." (Place the rope on the floor in a curvy line.)
- "Hop into the circle." (Form the rope into a circle on the floor.)
- "Tiptoe around the circle."

Add your own ideas for movement, or invite the children to suggest ways to move with the rope.

Hunt for Honey

Print the word "HONEY" on a piece of paper. Tape the paper onto a plastic jar. Ask one child to hide the "honey pot" while the other girls and boys cover their eyes. Then say, "Let's pretend to be busy little bees looking for our honey." The children can buzz around the room until one child finds the honey. The child who finds the honey can then hide it again.

Bible Craft Time
Make a River Scene

What you need:
- blue construction paper
- crayons
- o-shaped cereal
- pretzel sticks
- fish-shaped crackers
- canoe shapes cut from brown paper
- zip-lock bags (optional)

1st.... Encourage each child to glue a canoe onto a piece of blue paper.

2nd... Draw a person in the canoe.

3rd... Glue a pretzel stick in the person's hand for a fishing pole.

4th... Glue fish beneath the boat.

5th... Add o-shaped cereal for air bubbles.

6th... Draw a line from the fishing pole to one of the fish.

7th... Place a few leftover crackers, cereal, and pretzels in a zip-lock bag for each child. The child can shake the bag and then eat the river trail mix.

The Man Who Ate Bugs and Honey
Activity Sheet

Add each of the following to the picture to make it complete.
- Draw a leather belt around John the Baptist.
- Color the water blue.
- Draw the sun in the sky.
- Finish the plant and color it green.

Why Is Mary Doing That?

Do you have a brother or a sister?

The Bible tells about a woman named Mary. Mary had a sister named Martha. Mary and Martha lived in the same house together. One day, Jesus came to visit Mary and Martha. "Come in," said Martha. "I will fix us something to eat."

Jesus came into the house and sat down. Then Mary sat down beside Jesus' feet. Jesus started talking to Mary. Mary listened carefully to everything Jesus said.

Suddenly Martha came into the room. "Why is Mary doing that?" Martha asked Jesus. "I am doing all the work, and Mary is just sitting there. Tell Mary to help me."

Jesus looked up. "Martha," He said, "you are worried about so many things. But Mary is doing the right thing. She is listening to Me."

Another day, Jesus came to visit again. This time Jesus brought some of His friends with Him. While Jesus and His friends were eating supper, Mary came into the room. She was carrying a bottle of perfume.

Mary knelt down beside Jesus. She poured the perfume over Jesus' feet. Then she dried Jesus' feet with her hair. The whole house was filled with the beautiful smell of perfume.

Then Judas asked: "Why is Mary doing that? She should have sold the perfume and given the money to poor people."

But Jesus answered: "Leave Mary alone. She has done the right thing. Mary has shown Me that she loves Me."

From Luke 10:38-52; John 12:1-8

Bible Song Time
How Did Mary Show Her Love?
(tune "London Bridge")

Stand in a circle. Hold hands and swing arms as you sing.

How did Mary show her love, show her love, show her love?
How did Mary show her love for Jesus?

Cup your hands around your ears.
She listened to all He said, all He said, all He said.
She listened to all He said. She loved Jesus.

Pretend to pour perfume on your feet.
She poured perfume on His feet, on His feet, on His feet.
She poured perfume on His feet. She loved Jesus.

Bible Fun Time
Play a Listening Game

Ask the boys and girls to sit in a circle on the floor. Say: "Mary listened to everything Jesus said. In this game, we use our ears to listen, too." Then begin telling the children different actions to do. Use a different volume of your voice to say each action. For example, say:
- "If you are listening, nod your head." (loud voice)
- "If you are listening, tap your toes." (normal voice)
- "If you are listening, stand up." (loud voice)
- "If you are listening, turn around." (whisper)
- "If you are listening, clap three times." (normal voice)
- "If you are listening, reach up high." (soft voice)

Continue playing the game as long as the children are interested.

Play "Miss Lynn Says"

Ask the children to stand in a row. Explain: "Mary listened carefully to everything Jesus said. Today we will listen carefully while we play the game 'Miss Lynn Says' (use your own name in the game). Listen carefully to what I say. I will tell you something to do, such as, 'Miss Lynn says, "Wiggle your nose."' Then you can do what I said. But if I just say, 'Wiggle your nose,' don't do it. Wait till I say, 'Miss Lynn says, "Wiggle your nose."' Then give instructions such as:
- "Miss Lynn says, 'Reach up high.'"
- "Miss Lynn says, 'Turn around.'"
- "Miss Lynn says, 'Shake your head.'"

Once in awhile, give an instruction without saying, "Miss Lynn says." For instance, say, "Bend down low." If a child does the action anyway, just laugh and begin again.

Bible Craft Time
Make a Pretend Perfume Bottle

What you need:
- small, empty, soft drink bottles
- glue
- water
- aluminum pan or plastic bowl
- several colors of tissue paper
- paintbrushes
- paper towels

1st.... Mix one part glue and one part water in an aluminum pan or plastic bowl.

2nd... Invite each child to paint a plastic bottle with a thin coat of the glue mixture. Paint the entire bottle, except the bottom. Use a paper towel to wipe off any drips.

3rd... Stick pieces of tissue paper onto the bottle. Cover the entire bottle, except the bottom.

4th... Paint over the tissue paper with the glue mixture. Some colors may run together and form new colors.

Why Is Mary Doing That?
Activity Sheet

Remind the children, "Mary used her hair to dry Jesus' feet."
Look at each row of pictures.
Draw an X through the one that is different.

Why Is Mary Doing That?
Activity Sheet

Find and circle the

Matthew Follows Jesus

Do you have some money in a bank at home? The Bible tells about a man who collected people's money. Let's listen and find out what special thing happened to the man.

"One, two, three, four." Matthew was counting his money. Matthew worked in an office by the sea. He collected tax money from people.

Matthew looked up from his work. He saw a man walking along the seashore. Many people were following him. The man walked right up to the tax office and looked at Matthew. The man was Jesus!

"Follow Me!" Jesus said to Matthew.

So Matthew stood up and followed Jesus. Do you know where they went? Matthew and Jesus and many of the people following Jesus all went to Matthew's house! While they were there, they had a good time eating together.

Some men saw Jesus eating at Matthew's house. The men did not like Matthew. They did not like the other people Jesus was eating with either. The men thought the people were bad.

"Why is Jesus eating with all those bad people?" the men asked.

Jesus heard the men talking. "I have come to these people because they need Me," said Jesus. "These people need to know about God's love."

Matthew heard Jesus' answer. From that day on, Matthew followed Jesus.

From Mark 2:13-17

Bible Song Time
Matthew's Song
(tune "Happy Birthday to You")

Matthew followed Jesus. (walk in place)
Matthew followed Jesus.
Matthew learned about God's love. (cup hands to ears)
Matthew followed Jesus. (walk in place)

Matthew ate with Jesus. (pretend to eat)
Matthew ate with Jesus.
Matthew learned about God's love. (cup hands to ears)
Matthew ate with Jesus. (pretend to eat)

Bible Fun Time
Follow the Leader

If possible, go outside to play this game. Ask the children to walk behind you in a line and copy your actions.

If you can not go outside, ask the boys and girls to stand in a row. Stand facing the children, and invite them to copy your actions. Possible actions include:
- march like a soldier,
- hop on one foot,
- tiptoe,
- walk waving your arms over your head,
- walk with your arms flapping like birds' wings, and
- hop like a bunny.

Play a Guessing Game

Gather a roll of tape and several pictures of food items that will be familiar to the children. You can cut out food pictures from magazines, newspaper advertisements, and box or can labels. Or you can use crayons to draw simple sketches onto paper.

Place a loop of tape on the back of each picture. Remark: "Jesus ate food at Matthew's house. Let's play a guessing game about some of the food we like to eat."

Place a food picture on a child's back. Invite the boys and girls to give hints about the picture without actually naming it. For instance, for an banana picture, the children may tell that it is long, it is yellow, it grows on trees, and you peel it. You may need to prompt the preschoolers with questions such as "What color is it?" or "Where does it grow?" Continue giving hints until the child guesses which food is pictured. When the child names the food, show him the picture. Then place a picture on another child's back and begin again.

* Save the food pictures for use in a game with the next Bible story.

Bible Craft Time
Make a Coin Rubbing

You will need:
- cardboard
- glue or hot glue gun
- coins
- thin paper, such as typing paper
- crayons

1st.... Use glue or hot glue to attach several coins to pieces of cardboard.

2nd... Place a piece of paper on top of the coins.

3rd... Guide a child to rub a crayon onto the paper over a coin. An image of the coin will appear. Invite the child to rub over several coins.

4th... Remind the child: "Matthew used to collect money from people. But when Matthew saw Jesus, he left the money, and he followed Jesus."

Matthew Follows Jesus
Activity Sheet

Draw a line from each box to the matching coins.

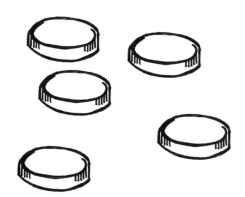 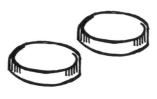 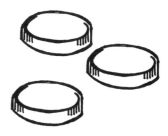

Matthew Follows Jesus
Activity Sheet

Draw a line from each item to where it belongs in the picture.

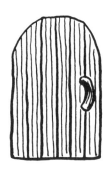

The Church That Shared

Have you or your parents ever brought an offering to church? Did you bring the money in an offering envelope? Did you put the money in the offering plate? People give money at church to help other people. The Bible tells about people who gave money at church. Let's find out who they were.

"Clink, clink, clink." Joseph heard the people giving money at church. Joseph knew the money would be used to help people.

"I want to help people, too," thought Joseph. "I will sell the land I own. Then I will bring the money to church."

So Joseph went out and sold his land. Then he hurried back to the church. When he saw the men collecting money, he walked over to them. Joseph gave the money to the men. He was so happy to share.

But Joseph's church was not the only one that helped others. Over in the city of Antioch, there was a church full of people who loved God.

One day a man came to the church. "I have some bad news," said the man. "Soon, people are not going to have enough food to eat. Many plants will stop growing. There will be no plants for food. People everywhere will be hungry."

The people at church wanted to help. So everyone brought some money to church. Then the people sent the money to their friends. With the money, their friends could buy some food. The people at church were happy to share and happy to help their friends.

From Acts 4:32, 36-37; 9:26-27; 11:22-30

Bible Song Time
The Sharing Song
(tune "Mulberry Bush")

Stand in a circle and hold hands. Swing your arms and smile as you sing.

People at church are happy to share,
They're happy to share,
They're happy to share.
People at church are happy to share,
They share with one another.

People at church are happy to share,
They're happy to share,
They're happy to share.
People at church are happy to share,
They share with other people.

Bible Fun Time
Pass the Offering Plate

Borrow an offering plate from the sanctuary, or locate an offering envelope or a basket that can be used as an offering basket. Prepare a cassette tape player or a record player to play music during the game.

Ask the children to sit on the floor in a circle. Say: "The Bible story told about people who gave money at church. At our church, we pass an offering plate so people can give money. Today we will pass the offering plate while the music plays. When the music stops, whoever has the offering plate can stand up."

Play the music and pass the offering plate. After it has gone around the circle once or twice, stop the music. When a child stands up with the plate, invite the child to start and stop the music as the game begins again.

Share Food Pictures

Gather several pictures of food. If you saved the pictures from the game with the last Bible story, use them. Cut each picture in half.

Ask the children to stand up and scatter around the room. Give each child a piece of a food picture. Say: "Today we heard that people at church shared with their friends so everyone could have food to eat. In this game, you have only half of a food picture. Find a friend who has the other half. You can both share your pieces to make a whole picture. When you find the friend with the matching piece, come sit beside me."

Sit down as the children walk around and find the matching food pictures. After all the children find their matches and sit down with you, let each pair show their completed picture to the group.

Bible Craft Time
Make Candy to Share

You will need:
- a hot mitt,
- a long-handled spoon,
- waxed paper,
- zip-lock bags,
- an electric skillet,
- an extension cord,
- 5-ounce can of chow mein noodles,
- 12-ounce bag of chocolate chips

1st.... Turn the skillet on 175 degrees. Remind the children not to touch the hot skillet. Supervise carefully.

2nd... Invite a child to pour the chocolate chips into the skillet.

3rd... Allow the children to take turns wearing the hot mitt and stirring the chips.

4th... When the chips have melted, invite a child to pour in the noodles while another child stirs.

5th... Guide each child to spoon out several small scoops of candy onto the waxed paper.

6th... When the candy cools, allow each child to eat one piece.

7th... Place the remaining pieces of candy in a zip-lock bag.

8th... Share the candy with the pastor, with the church choir, or with another church helper.

The Church That Shared
Activity Sheet

Write 1 or • in the circle to show what happened first.
Write 2 or •• in the circle to show what happened second.
Write 3 or ••• in the circle to show what happened third.
Write 4 or •••• in the circle to show what happened fourth.

The Church That Shared
Activity Sheet

Finish the picture.
- Draw coins in the basket.
- Color the money pouch brown.
- Finish drawing the table.

We Choose Stephen

Has your mother or father ever asked for your help? How did it feel to be a helper? The Bible tells about a man who was chosen to be a helper. Let's listen and find out where he helped.

"Everyone come over here!" called some men at the church.

All the people hurried over to the men. Stephen went, too. He wanted to hear what the men were going to say.

"We need someone to help us with the work at church," said the men. "Please, choose seven helpers. They can do part of the work."

"That's a good idea," thought Stephen. "I wonder who the people will choose."

"We need someone who loves God," said the people. "We need someone who will do a good job."

The people thought and thought. Then they started naming the seven men they had chosen. "And we choose Stephen," said the people.

What a surprise! Stephen was happy to be chosen. He was glad to be a church helper. Stephen did many wonderful things to help the people, and he told the people about Jesus.

"Stephen is a good helper," said the people. "We are glad that we chose Stephen."

From Acts 6:3-5a, 6, 8-15, 7:58-60

Bible Song Time
Stephen Was a Helper
(tune "Mary Had a Little Lamb")

Stephen was a helper, helper, helper.
Stephen was a helper, a helper at his church.

After singing the first stanza, invite a child to stand up.
Use the child's name in the song as everyone sings:

Lauren is a helper, helper, helper.
Lauren is a helper, a helper at our church.
Let the child choose a friend to stand next.

Bible Fun Time
Play a Guessing Game

Gather several items the children use at church, such as a pair of blunt-pointed scissors, a crayon, a small block, and a plastic dish. Put the items in a sack so the children cannot see them.

Sit in a circle on the floor. Invite one child to sit in front of you with her back to you. Ask the child to place her hands behind her back. Say: "I am going to put something in your hands. It is something you use at church. Try to guess what it is without looking at it. Just feel of it and see if you know what it is."

Place an item in her hand. If she does not guess what it is, give hints such as: "It is made of wood. You build with it."

When the child guesses correctly, give a turn to someone else. Continue playing until every child has had a turn.

Bible Craft Time
Make a Helping Hands Picture

You will need:
- construction paper
- paper plates
- scissors
- glue
- hole punch
- yarn or ribbon cut into 18-inch lengths (1 length per child)
- pencil
- felt-tip marker
- masking tape

1st .... Wrap masking tape around one end of each yarn piece.

2nd ... Fold the sheets of construction paper in half.

3rd ... Guide a child to place his left hand on top of the folded paper with his little finger and wrist along the folded edge.

4th ... Trace around the fingers and hand with a pencil. Start at the top of the little finger and continue all the way around to the wrist at the bottom of the thumb.

5th ... Cut around the hand print through both layers of paper, except for the folded edge.

6th ... Invite the child to unfold the hand print and glue it onto a paper plate.

7th ... Print "I can help at church" on the hand print. As you print, talk about ways the child can help at church, such as put toys away, throw away trash, and wipe off a table.

8th ... Show the child how to punch holes around the edge of the paper plate.

9th ... Guide the child to start at the top center of the plate and thread the yarn through the holes.

10th .. Tie excess yarn into a bow.

We Choose Stephen
Activity Sheet

How can you be a helper at church? Draw a line from each picture on the left to a picture on the right that shows how you can help at church.

We Choose Stephen
Activity Sheet

Stephen helped at church.
Connect the dots to finish Stephen's robe.

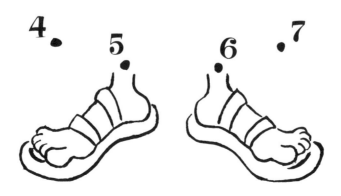

The Tent Makers

Have you ever been inside a tent? Did you sleep in the tent? The Bible tells about two people who made tents. But these two people did something else, also. Let's listen and find out what they did.

"This one is finished," said Aquila as he sewed the last stitches into the heavy material.

"It will be a good tent," nodded Priscilla, his wife. "I'm glad you're through sewing it, because now it's time for us to go on our trip to Ephesus."

Aquila and Priscilla walked together to the boat dock. They climbed on board the big sail boat. Then they rode the boat across the sea.

When they landed at Ephesus, Aquila and Priscilla went to the church. They heard a man named Apollos talking about Jesus.

"Come over here, Apollos," said Aquila and Priscilla. "We want to help you. We will teach you more things about Jesus."

Apollos went over to Aquila and Priscilla. He listened to them. He learned many things about Jesus from Aquila and Priscilla.

So Aquila and Priscilla were not only tent makers, they were teachers, too!

From Acts 18:1-4, 18-19, 24-26; Romans 16:3-5a

Bible Song Time
Aquila and Priscilla
(tune "Mulberry Bush")

This is the way they sewed the tent, (pretend to sew)
Sewed the tent, sewed the tent.
This is the way they sewed the tent,
Aquila and Priscilla.

This is the way they rode a boat, (move hand like an ocean wave)
Rode a boat, rode a boat.
This is the way they rode a boat,
Aquila and Priscilla.

This is the way they said, "Come here," (make a "come here" motion)
Said, "Come here," Said, "Come here." (with hand and arm)
This is the way they said, "Come here,"
Aquila and Priscilla.

Bible Fun Time
Come Over Here

Ask the children to stand on one side of the room while you stand on the other side. Comment: "In today's Bible story, Aquila and Priscilla told Apollo to 'Come over here.' In this game, I will tell you who can come over here to me. Listen carefully to hear when to come." Then give instructions such as:

- If you have on blue shoes, tiptoe to me.
- If you have on a white shirt, hop to me.
- If you have brown eyes, walk backwards to me.

When all the children have come to you, move to another part of the room and begin again.

Can You Learn?

Guide the girls and boys to stand in a circle. Remark: "Today's Bible story tells us that Apollos learned about Jesus. Now let's play an action game to see what we can learn."

Ask the following questions. Encourage the children to make the motions with you.

- Can you learn to turn around three times?
- Can you learn to hop on just one foot?
- Can you learn to tap your toes while you clap your hands?
- Can you learn to rub your head and your tummy at the same time?
- Can you learn to raise your right hand and your left foot at the same time?
- Can you learn to put your hands on your head while you sit down?

Bible Craft Time
Make a Seascape

You will need:
- a cake pan with a clear lid
- brown or white paper, or brown paper grocery bags
- scissors
- blue paint
- green paint
- marbles or golf balls
- spoons
- plastic bowls

1st.... Trim pieces of paper to fit in the bottom of the cake pan. If you use brown grocery bags, flatten them out and cut them into sheets that will fit in the pan.

2nd... Pour the blue paint into one bowl and the green paint into another bowl.

3rd... Place several marbles or golf balls and a spoon in each bowl.

4th... Write the child's name on the back of a piece of paper.

5th... Place the paper in the cake pan.

6th... Invite a child to use the spoons to put several blue paint marbles and several green paint marbles in the pan.

7th... Put the lid on the pan.

8th... Show the child how to hold the pan and gently rock it back and forth.

9th... When the child is through, remove the lid and place the marbles back into the paint.

10th.. Take out the paper to dry.

The Tent Makers
Activity Sheet

Look at the pictures in each row.
Circle the 2 pictures that are the same.

   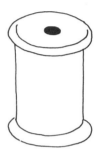

 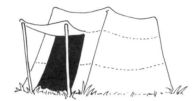 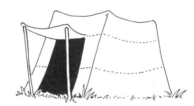 

The Tent Makers
Activity Sheet

Cut along the dotted lines to separate the four puzzle pieces.
Arrange the pieces to form a boat. Paste the boat onto another piece of paper.
OPTION: Paste the boat onto a piece of cardboard. Punch holes around the pictures.
Sew through the holes with yarn.

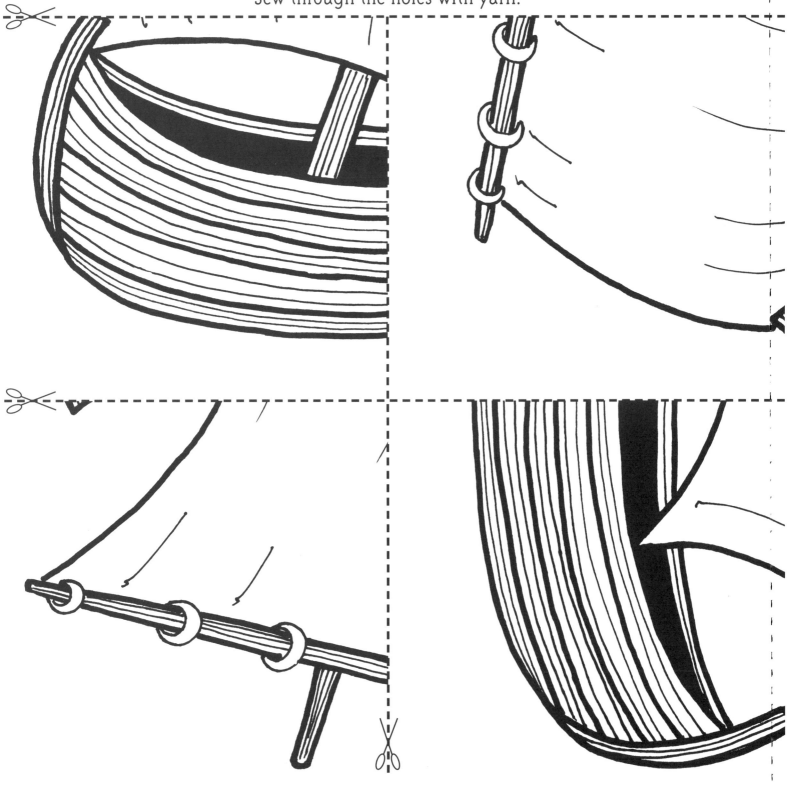

Timothy Two Ears

How many ears do you have? What do we do with our ears? What is your favorite sound to hear?

Long ago there lived a little boy named Timothy. Timothy was a child just like you. He had two eyes, he had one nose, and he had two ears. Timothy could hear many things with his two ears. One of his favorite things to hear was a Bible story.

Timothy's mother and grandmother told him many Bible stories. They told Timothy how much God loved him.

Every day Timothy grew and grew, and every day he learned about God. As he grew, Timothy learned to love God. He learned to do what was right.

When Timothy grew to be a young man, he traveled with a man named Paul. Everywhere they traveled, Timothy and Paul told people about God.

One day Paul told Timothy: "Your mother and grandmother taught you many things about God. Remember all the things they taught you. Keep doing the things you learned."

Timothy did remember the things his mother and grandmother taught him. Timothy went many places teaching other people about God, too.

From Acts 16:1-3; 2 Timothy 1:1-5; 3:14-15

Bible Song Time
Hearing Ears
(tune "Are You Sleeping?")

A teacher can sing a phrase and have the children echo it.
Or, if you prefer, everyone can sing the whole song together.

Where are your ears? Where are your ears?
Here is one. Here is one. (point to one ear)
Where is the other? Where is the other?
Here is two. Here is two. (point to the other ear)

What do we hear? What do we hear?
With our ears? With our ears? (point to one ear)
We hear Bible stories. We hear Bible stories.
With our ears. With our ears. (point to the other ear)

Bible Fun Time
I Know Someone God Loves

Explain: "I'm going to describe someone God loves. When you think you know the person I'm describing, stand up and raise your hand."

When all the children understand how to play, say: "I know someone God loves. The person's name begins with the letter D. The person has on black shoes. The person is wearing a bracelet." Keep describing the person until a child stands up and raises his hand to guess.

Ask, "Do you know who God loves?" If the child does not guess the person you had in mind, continue describing until someone guesses the person you meant. When a child guesses correctly, begin again by describing another preschooler. Continue playing until you have described every child.

What Do You Hear?

Collect six empty film canisters or empty spice bottles. Put sand, sugar, or salt in one container. In the other containers, put rice, water, a coin, a rock, and a cotton ball.

Shake a container and encourage the boys and girls to guess what is inside. You may need to give clues such as: "You find it outside on the ground. It is hard."

When a child guesses correctly, open the container and show everyone. The shake another container.

The cotton ball will not make a sound. Give clues such as: "It is round and soft and white. You might have some in your bathroom at home. It looks like a little white cloud."

Be prepared! Preschoolers usually ask to play this game again!

Bible Craft Time
Make a Self-Portrait

You will need:
- paper
- large oval shapes for faces
- small oval shapes for ears
- crayons or washable felt-tip markers
- glue
- unbreakable hand mirror

1st.... Invite a child to glue a large oval onto a piece of paper.

2nd... Guide the child to add two small ovals for ears.

3rd... Show the child her reflection in the mirror. Point out the child's eye color and hair color.

4th... Encourage the child to complete her self-portrait by drawing eyes, nose, mouth, and hair with the crayons or markers.

5th... At the top of the paper, print the child's name. At the bottom of the paper, print, "Hears About God's Love."

Timothy Two Ears
Activity Sheet

Where do I hear about God?
Draw lines to connect the matching pictures.

Timothy Two Ears
Activity Sheet

Circle each thing that makes a sound you can hear.

Two Brave Men

Who is the bravest person you know? Has there ever been a time when you needed to be brave?

The Bible tells about two very brave men. Their names were Paul and Silas. Everywhere Paul and Silas went, they told people about Jesus. Some of the people were happy to hear about Jesus. But other people did not want to hear about Him. They became angry with Paul and Silas. Sometimes they hurt Paul and Silas and threw them in jail.

But Paul and Silas were brave men. They kept on telling everyone about Jesus.

One day Paul and Silas traveled to a town called Thessalonica. They walked into the church and started reading the Bible. They told all the people about Jesus. Then they went to stay at their friend Jason's house.

Soon some men came to Jason's house. "Give us Paul and Silas!" they yelled. "We do not like the things they are teaching."

But Paul and Silas did not go with the men. Paul and Silas left Thessalonica that night. They traveled to another town. And do you know what Paul and Silas did as soon as they came to the new town? They started telling people about Jesus! Paul and Silas were two very brave men.

From Acts 17:2-5, 10; 1 Thessalonians 2:1-2, 10-12

Bible Song Time
Paul and Silas
(tune "Mulberry Bush")

Paul and Silas went to church, (walk in place)
Went to church, went to church.
Paul and Silas went to church,
To teach about Jesus.

Paul and Silas read the Bible, (hold hands together as if reading a book)
Read the Bible, read the Bible.
Paul and Silas read the Bible,
To teach about Jesus.

Paul and Silas were brave men, (make fist; punch up into air)
Were brave men, were brave men.
Paul and Silas were brave men,
To teach about Jesus.

Bible Fun Time
Pass the Beanbag

Locate a beanbag. Or fill a sock halfway with dry beans and tie a double knot to close the sock.

Ask the girls and boys to stand in a circle. Comment: "Paul and Silas worked together to tell people about Jesus. We can work together, too. We will try to pass this beanbag all the way around the circle. Work together to carefully pass the beanbag." Try the following ways of passing the beanbag:

- Put your right hand on your head, and pass the beanbag with your left hand.
- Pinch the beanbag with two fingers. Pass the beanbag using only these two fingers.
- Turn with your backs facing the inside of the circle. Pass the beanbag behind your backs.
- Turn sideways so that you face each other's backs. Bend down and pass the beanbag through your legs.
- Continue to stand sideways. Pass the beanbag over your shoulders.

The children may also think of ways to pass the beanbag. Each time they complete the circle, say: "You worked together!"

Working Together

Gather a flat sheet and a beach ball. Encourage the children to work together to make the ball go high into the air and then catch it again. Also, see if the children can make the ball roll around on the sheet without letting it fall off.

Bible Craft Time
Make a Footsteps Painting

You will need:
- paper
- liquid tempera paint
- old shoes of various sizes
- paper towels
- plastic dishpan
- painting smocks

1st . . . . Fold some paper towels into a thick pad.

2nd . . . Pour paint into the dishpan, just enough to cover the bottom.

3rd . . . Put a painting smock on a child.

4th . . . Guide the child to hold the top of a shoe and carefully dip the sole in paint.

5th . . . Press the shoe onto the paper towels to remove excess paint.

6th . . . Make a shoe print on the paper.

7th . . . Repeat the process with other shoes.

8th . . . As a child works, say: "Paul and Silas walked many places telling people about Jesus." Talk about the different people. Who might have worn the shoes you are using? Were they adults or children? Men or women? Add: "We can all tell people about Jesus. You can tell people about Jesus, too."

Two Brave Men
Activity Sheet

Color and cut out the door knocker.
Glue the door knocker onto thin cardboard or construction paper.
Cut out again and hang the knocker on a friend's door.

Two Brave Men
Activity Sheet

Help Paul and Silas find their way to church.

Something New

How do your parents show that they love you? How do you show that you love your parents?

One day, Jesus told His friends about love. Jesus and His friends were sitting together in an upstairs room. They had just finished eating supper.

Suddenly, Jesus said: "Everyone listen to Me. I have something new to tell you. I have never told you this before."

Everyone looked at Jesus. What was He going to say? Everyone wanted to hear.

"I want you all to love one another," said Jesus. "I have loved you. Now you love one another. People will know that you are My friends, if you love one another."

Jesus' friends did what He said. They loved one another. They taught other people to love one another, too.

From John 13:34-35; 1 Thessalonians 4:1-2, 9-10

Bible Song Time
Love One Another
(tune "Jesus Loves Me" chorus)

Stand in a circle. Hold hands and swing arms as you sing.

Love one another.
Love one another.
Love one another.
This is the happy way.

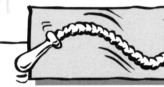 

Bible Fun Time
Showing Love

Say: "Loving one another is not just a feeling. It is something you do. Let's do an action song about ways we can show love."

Use motions to illustrate each action as you sing the following words to the tune "Mulberry Bush":
"This is the way we wash the dishes,
Wash the dishes, wash the dishes.
This is the way we wash the dishes
When we love one another."

Other stanzas include:
"This is the way we water the plants."
"This is the way we sweep the floor."
"This is the way we dust furniture."
"This is the way we give a hug."

Also encourage the children to name ways they show love. Sing about the ways the children name.

Bible Craft Time
Make a Stained Glass Heart

You will need:
- small paper plates
- scissors
- pencil
- different colors of tissue paper
- clear contact plastic
- hole punch
- yarn or ribbon

1st....Draw a heart shape on the back of each plate.

2nd...Cut out the heart shapes.

3rd...On the paper side of the contact plastic, draw circles that will completely cover the heart shapes.

4th...Cut out the circles.

5th...Remove the paper backing from a circle.

6th...Place the circle on the plate so the sticky side shows through the bottom of the plate.

7th...Onto the bottom of the plate, press the paper circle that you peeled off the plastic.

8th...Prepare the other plates in the same manner. Stack the plates together.

9th...Cut the tissue paper into small pieces.

10th..Give a plate to a child.

11th...Remove the paper backing.

12th...Invite the child to put pieces of tissue paper on the sticky plastic until the heart is completely covered.

13th..Punch a hole at the top edge of the plate.

14th..Tie a piece of yarn or ribbon through the hole.

Something New
Activity Sheet

Who is showing love?
Circle the children who are showing love.
Draw an X through the children who are not showing love.
Remind the children, "Jesus said for us to love one another."

Something New
Activity Sheet

What would Jesus want you to do?
Draw a line from each picture on the left to the picture on the right that shows how a child can show love.

A Very Special Supper

Have you ever helped your parents fix supper? What part did you do?

One day Jesus asked Peter and John to fix a special supper. "Where can we fix the supper?" asked Peter and John.

"Go into the city," said Jesus. "You will see a man carrying a pitcher of water. Follow the man to his house. He will take you upstairs to a room where you can fix the supper."

Peter and John did what Jesus said. They found the man carrying the pitcher of water. "Where can we fix supper for Jesus?" they asked.

The man took Peter and John to a room upstairs. "You can fix the supper here," he said.

When the supper was ready, Jesus and His friends came to eat. Jesus gave everyone something to drink and prayed, "Thank You, God, for giving us good things to drink."

Then Jesus took some bread and prayed, "Thank You, God, for giving us food to eat."

Then Jesus gave everyone a piece of bread. "I want you to always remember this special supper," said Jesus. "I want you to always remember Me. Remember that I love you."

From Luke 22:8-20; 2 Thessalonians 1:4-5

Bible Song Time
Jesus' Special Supper
(tune "Happy Birthday")

Jesus went upstairs (pretend to walk up steps)
Jesus went upstairs.
For His special supper,
Jesus went upstairs.

Jesus said thank you. (fold hands in prayer)
Jesus said thank you.
For His special supper,
Jesus said thank you.

Jesus ate good food. (pretend to eat)
Jesus ate good food.
For His special supper,
Jesus ate good food.

Bible Fun Time
Do You Remember?

Gather four or five food items. For instance, gather a potato, an apple, an orange, a banana, and a carrot. Ask the children to sit in a circle on the floor. Say: "The Bible story today told us that Jesus ate food with His friends. Jesus told His friends to remember Him. Now we will play a food game where we try to remember."

Lay the food items in front of you. Point to each item as you name it. Then cover the items with a towel.

Encourage the boys and girls to close their eyes as you reach beneath the towel and remove an item. When the item is behind your back, say, "Open your eyes!"

Lift the towel and see if the children can name the missing item. Replace the item and begin again.

Water Play

Say: "Jesus told His friends to find a man carrying a pitcher of water. What do you think the man was going to do with the water?"

Invite each child to play out something you can do with water. A preschooler may need you to suggest something for him to play out, such as swimming, drinking, bathing, washing dishes, washing hair, watering plants, or washing the car. The other girls and boys can guess what the child is pretending to do.

Bible Craft Time
Make a Bible Time Home

You will need:
- small cardboard boxes such as facial tissue boxes (1 per child)
- smaller cardboard boxes such as bar soap boxes (1 per child)
- paper
- brown grocery bags
- glue sticks or paste
- scissors
- crayons or washable felt-tip markers

1st.... If your boxes have anything printed on the outside, cut out squares of paper to fit the sides and the tops of the boxes. Paper from brown grocery bags works well for this step.

2nd... Cut out small squares and rectangles for doors and windows.

3rd... Cut out strips of paper one inch wide and fold them accordion-style to form steps.

4th... Guide a child to glue paper squares on the sides and top of a box of each size.

5th... Show the child how to glue the smaller box on top of the bigger one.

6th... Help the child glue the steps on one side of the bottom box so they extend from the floor to the roof.

7th... Let the child glue windows and doors on both boxes.

8th... Invite the child to put finishing touches on the house with crayons or markers.

A Very Special Supper
Activity Sheet

Draw a line from each food to its matching shadow.

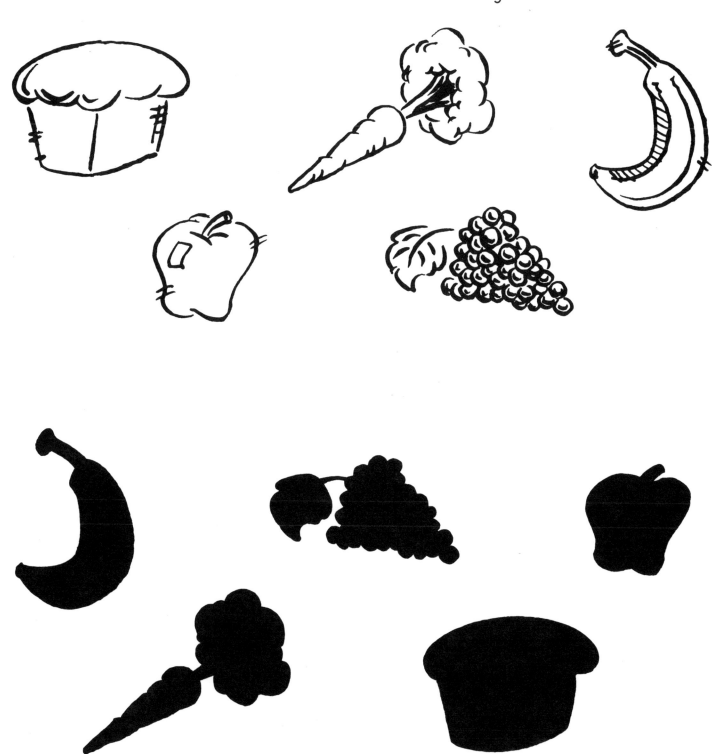

A Very Special Supper
Activity Sheet

Cut along the dotted lines to separate the pictures.
Glue the pictures onto a piece of paper in the order they happened.

The Day the Children Sang

How did you come to church today? Did you ride in a car?

One day Jesus and His friends were walking to the church in Jerusalem. Suddenly, Jesus said: "Go to the next town. You will find a donkey tied there. Untie the donkey and bring it to Me."

So Jesus' friends went to the town. They found the donkey and took it to Jesus. The donkey did not have a saddle, so Jesus' friends laid their coats over the donkey's back. Then Jesus sat down on the donkey. He started riding the donkey into Jerusalem.

The people were so happy to see Jesus. Some people laid their coats in the road for the donkey to walk on. Other people cut branches from trees. They laid the branches in the road. Everyone was shouting and singing: "We love You, Jesus! You are God's Son!"

Finally Jesus arrived at church. He climbed off the donkey and walked into the church building. Many people who could not walk and many people who could not see were at the church that day.

"Please help us," said the people. "We want to see. We want to walk."

So Jesus helped the people. He made the blind people see. He made the crippled people walk.

Many children were also at the temple. The children started singing: "We love You, Jesus. Hosanna to Jesus."

Then some men walked up to Jesus. "Do you hear those children?" asked the men. "Make them stop singing!"

"I will not make the children stop singing," said Jesus. "They are doing the right thing. They are singing praise to Me."

From Matthew 21:1-11, 14-16; 2 Thessalonians 3:1

Bible Song Time
A Praise Song
(tune "Are You Sleeping?")

A teacher can sing a phrase and have the children echo it.
Or, if you prefer, everyone can sing the whole song together.

Hosanna. Hosanna.
To Jesus. To Jesus.
Jesus is God's Son. Jesus is God's Son.
We love Him. We love Him.

Bible Fun Time
Going for a Walk

Guide the children to stand in a circle. Explain: "Jesus and His friends usually walked to church. Sometimes they had to walk a long way. Let's pretend we are going on a long walk, too." Then say:

- "I'm going for a walk."   (walk in place)
- "I hop over a rock."   (give a little hop)
- "I pass by a tree."   (wave arms like tree branches)
- "I listen to a bee."   (cup hands at ears and buzz)
- "I clap at a fly."   (clap hands in air)
- "I watch clouds float by." (cup hands around eyes like binoculars)
- "Whew! I'm tired now."   (wipe hand across brow)
- "I think I will sit down." (sit on floor)

Bible Craft Time
Make a Bible Time Home

You will need:
- tape
- waxed paper
- plastic wrap
- leaves
- felt-tip markers or water colors
- 1 cup cornstarch
- 1 one-pound box baking soda
- 1 1/2 cups water

1st.... Mix cornstarch and baking soda in saucepan.

2nd... Gradually add water.

3rd... Cook over low heat, stirring constantly. The mixture will bubble, thicken, and finally form a ball.

4th... When mixture forms a ball, remove from heat. Empty onto plastic wrap and allow to cool completely. Mixture will continue to thicken as it cools.

5th... Wrap tightly in plastic wrap and refrigerate until day of use. Bring clay to room temperature before using it.

6th... Cover work surface with waxed paper and tape into place.

7th... Roll a piece of clay into a ball and place it on the waxed paper.

8th... Guide a child to flatten the ball with the palm of his hand until it is about 1/2-inch thick.

9th... Invite the child to place a leaf on top of the clay.

10th.. Guide the child to press the leaf into the clay and then carefully remove it.

11th... Encourage the child to carefully color the imprint with markers or water colors. The imprint will harden overnight.

12th... Comment: "The leaf imprint reminds us that people laid tree branches in the road for Jesus to ride over."

The Day the Children Sang
Activity Sheet

Circle the picture that answers each question.

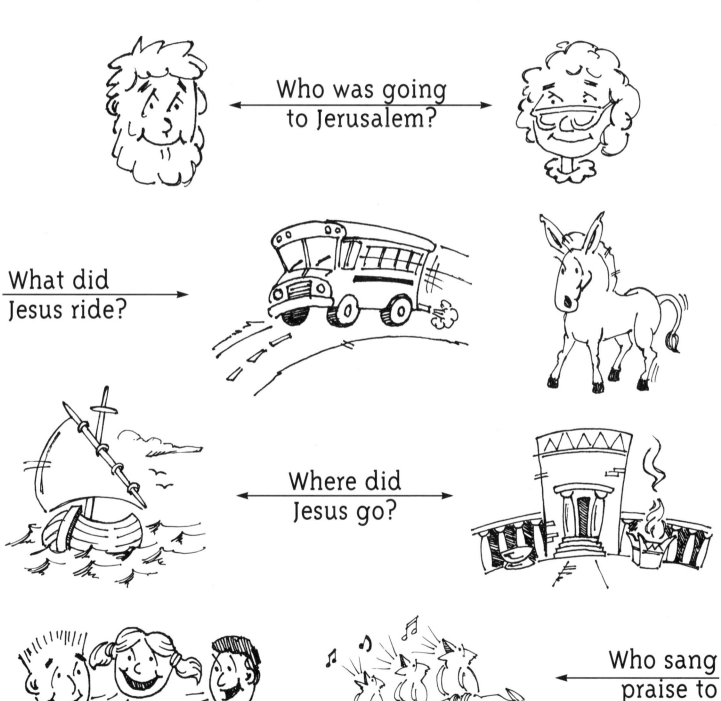

The Day the Children Sang
Activity Sheet

Color the tree branches green.
Cut out the branches.
Glue them on the road in front of Jesus.

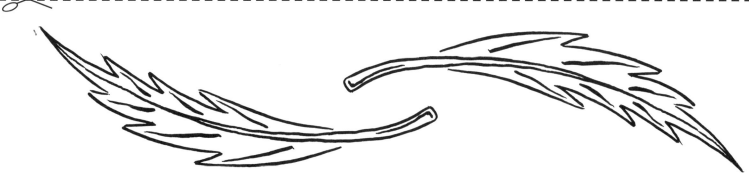

The Very First Easter

How do you feel when you wake up on Easter day? The Bible tells us about the very first Easter day. Let's listen and find out why it is such a special day.

Flip, flap, flip, flap, sounded Mary's sandals as she and the other women walked down the dusty road. It was early Sunday morning. The sun was just barely beginning to come up.

Mary felt very sad as she walked along. She and the women were on their way to the place where Jesus had been buried.

When Mary and the women came to the grave, they saw that the heavy stone door had been rolled open. And do you know what they saw sitting on top of the stone door? They saw an angel! The women felt very frightened.

"Do not be afraid," said the angel. "Jesus is not here. He is alive."

The women were so excited!. They ran back down the road. They wanted to tell everyone what the angel said.

Suddenly, the women saw someone walking toward them. It was Jesus! Jesus was alive! The women were so happy to see Jesus.

"Go tell My friends that you have seen Me," said Jesus. "Tell them that I am alive. Tell them that they will see Me soon."

From Matthew 28:1-10; 1 Thessalonians 4:13-18

Bible Song Time
Happy Easter Day
(tune "The Bear Went Over the Mountain")

Stand in a circle and hold hands. Walk in a ring as you sing.

O, happy, happy Easter.

O, happy, happy Easter.

O, happy, happy Easter,

For Jesus is alive! (raise arms over head)

Walk in the other direction.

O, happy, happy Easter.

O, happy, happy Easter.

O, happy, happy Easter,

For Jesus loves us so! (raise arms over head)

Bible Fun Time
I Spy a Friend

Locate an empty cardboard tube such as from a roll of paper towels.

Explain: "In our Bible story today, Mary saw a friend who made her happy. Mary saw Jesus. Today we will play a game looking at friends who make us happy. See if you can guess who my friend is."

Look through the cardboard tube as if it were a telescope. Look at one of the children. Say: "I spy a friend who makes me happy. The friend has on a blue dress. The friend has brown, curly hair." Continue giving hints until someone guesses correctly. Then begin again, describing another child. Be sure every child is described.

Older preschoolers may enjoy looking through the tube and describing a friend for the others to guess.

Make an Easter Discovery

Use tape or glue to secure a mirror inside a shoe box or other box with a lid. Comment: "Inside this box, you will see someone that Jesus loves." Demonstrate how to peek inside the box.

Pass the box around the circle and give every child an opportunity to look inside. Each child will see his own reflection in the mirror.

When the box returns to you, remark: "Who does Jesus love? Jesus loves you!"

Bible Craft Time
Make an Easter Shaker

You will need:
- heavy paper plates
- ice pick
- chenille sticks
- jingle bells
- scissors
- crayons

1st.... Cut chenille sticks into three-inch lengths.

2nd... Use the ice pick to poke two holes about one inch apart in a plate.

3rd... Invite a child to thread a bell onto a piece of chenille stick.

4th... Guide the child to insert one end of the stick into one hole and the other end of the stick into the second hole. Twist the ends so the bell is secured to the plate.

5th... Attach several more bells to the plate.

6th... Decorate the plate with crayons.

7th... Say: "People like to sing and play instruments at Easter because they are so happy. Do you remember why Easter is a happy day? That's right, because Jesus is alive."

The Very First Easter
Activity Sheet

Finish drawing Mary's face to show how she felt in the story.

How did Mary feel when she was walking down the road?

How did Mary feel when she saw the angel?

How did Mary feel when she saw Jesus?

How do you feel on Easter Sunday?

The Very First Easter
Activity Sheet

Finish the picture.
Draw the stone rolled away.
Draw petals on the flowers.
Trace the words "Jesus is alive!"

JESUS IS ALIVE!